THROUGH FAITH AND FLAWS

A 30-Day Journal with Women of the Old Testament

Friendship Press®

Friendship Press
P.O. Box 117
Wyncote, PA 19095

Library of Congress Catalog-in-Publication data available upon request

ISBN (hardcover): 978-1-961088-13-9

Verse selection and prompts by Beth Ann Gaede
Cover and interior design by Laurie Ingram

Typesetting by Integra Software Services Pvt. Ltd.
Printed in the United States of America

About This Journal

Throughout Scripture we see God at work in twists, puzzles, and surprises. God asked the tongue-tied Moses to lead the Hebrew people to the promised land. God appointed the young shepherd David to be king of Israel. God chose the unwed Mary to be the mother of the Messiah. God's resurrected Son, Jesus, presented himself to Mary Magdalene three days after his crucifixion.

In this collection of passages and reflections on women of the Old Testament, we see God at work through women who were faithful and women who were deeply flawed, even evil. And we see that some women were both faithful and flawed. On this thirty-day journey, consider ways you are like these God-chosen women—and ways God uses you, your whole person, to witness to God's reconciling love for all creation.

Each *NRSVue Bible Journal* is offered with the hope that you will be inspired by your encounter with scripture and that journaling becomes a helpful part of your devotional journey.

The undated pages allow you to write at your own pace, with scripture passages and thoughtful writing prompts placed at regular intervals for you to meditate on, pray over, and write about as the Spirit moves you.

date

GENESIS 1:26–27, 31

EVE

Then God said, "Let us make humans in our image, according to our likeness. . . ."

So God created humans in his image,

  in the image of God he created them;

  male and female he created them. . . .

God saw everything that he had made, and indeed, it was very good.

date

In spite of natural disasters, human suffering, and the evil people commit, in what ways is God's creation very good?

date

GENESIS 2:18, 21–23

EVE

Then the LORD God said, "It is not good that the man should be alone; I will make him a helper as his partner." . . . So the LORD God caused a deep sleep to fall upon the man, and he slept; then he took one of his ribs and closed up its place with flesh. And the rib that the LORD God had taken from the man he made into a woman and brought her to the man. Then the man said,

"This at last is bone of my bones
    and flesh of my flesh."

date

Do you think the interconnectedness of God's creation extends beyond human beings? Why or why not?

date

date

date

GENESIS 2:25; 3:7, 21

EVE

And the man and his wife were both naked and were not ashamed. . . . Then the eyes of both were opened, and they knew that they were naked, and they sewed fig leaves together and made loincloths for themselves. . . . And the LORD God made garments of skins for the man and for his wife and clothed them.

date

How does Adam and Eve's nakedness and clothing reflect the changing nature of their relationship with God? How has your own faith changed over the years?

date

date

date

GENESIS 18:1–2, 10, 12

SARAH

The LORD appeared to Abraham by the oaks of Mamre, as he sat at the entrance of his tent in the heat of the day. He looked up and saw three men standing near him. . . .

Then one said, "I will surely return to you in due season, and your wife Sarah shall have a son." And Sarah was listening at the tent entrance behind him. . . . So Sarah laughed to herself, saying, "After I have grown old, and my husband is old, shall I be fruitful?"

date

Did Sarah's skepticism about the man's promise demonstrate wisdom based on experience or a lack of faith? When has your own trust in God been challenged?

date

GENESIS 21:1–3, 6
SARAH

The LORD dealt with Sarah as he had said. . . . Sarah conceived and bore Abraham a son in his old age. . . . Abraham gave the name Isaac to his son whom Sarah bore him. . . . Now Sarah said, "God has brought laughter for me; everyone who hears will laugh with me."

date

The name Isaac means "one who laughs" or "one who rejoices." What Isaacs—reasons for joy—has God given you?

date

date

date

GENESIS 21:14, 17–18

HAGAR

So Abraham rose early in the morning and took bread and a skin of water and gave it to Hagar, putting it on her shoulder, along with the child [Ishmael], and sent her away. And she departed and wandered about in the wilderness of Beer-sheba. . . .

And the angel of God called to Hagar from heaven and said to her, . . . "Come, lift up the boy and hold him fast with your hand, for I will make a great nation of him."

date

What feelings do you imagine welled up in Hagar as she wandered in the wilderness? When have you been given a surprising reason to hope?

date

date

date

GENESIS 25:24, 27–28

REBEKAH

When her [Rebekah's] time to give birth was at hand, there were twins in her womb. . . . When the boys grew up, Esau was a skillful hunter, a man of the field, while Jacob was a quiet man, living in tents. Isaac [Rebekah's husband] loved Esau because he was fond of game, but Rebekah loved Jacob.

date

The tension between Rebekah's sons provides a compelling storyline. What does this element of intrigue add to our understanding of God?

date

GENESIS 30:1, 22–23

RACHEL

When Rachel saw that she bore Jacob no children, she envied her sister, and she said to Jacob, "Give me children, or I shall die!" . . . Then God remembered Rachel, and God heeded her and opened her womb. She conceived and bore a son.

date

Rachel had difficulty conceiving a child, but Jewish tradition calls her "the mother of Israel." What ironies, twists, or surprises have you experienced in your walk with God?

date

date

date

GENESIS 39:6–8, 11–12, 16–17

POTIPHAR'S WIFE

Now Joseph was handsome and good-looking. And after a time his master's wife cast her eyes on Joseph and said, "Lie with me." But he refused. . . . One day, however, when he went into the house to do his work, and while no one else was in the house, she caught hold of his garment, saying, "Lie with me!" But he left his garment in her hand and fled and ran outside. . . . Then she kept his garment by her until his master came home, and she told him the same story.

date

When have you experienced deep betrayal? How have you found a path toward growth and healing at such times?

date

date

date

EXODUS 2:1–4

JOCHEBED AND MIRIAM

Now a man from the house of Levi went and married a Levite woman [Jochebed]. The woman conceived and bore a son, and when she saw that he was a fine baby, she hid him three months. When she could hide him no longer she got a papyrus basket for him and plastered it with bitumen and pitch; she put the child in it and placed it among the reeds on the bank of the river. His sister [Miriam] stood at a distance, to see what would happen to him.

date

When have you made a leap of faith that required you to wait "to see what would happen"? In what ways was waiting difficult? How were you changed by the leap?

date

EXODUS 2:5–6, 10

PHARAOH'S DAUGHTER

The daughter of Pharaoh came down to bathe at the river, while her attendants walked beside the river. She saw the basket among the reeds and sent her maid to bring it. When she opened it, she saw the child. He was crying, and she took pity on him. . . . When the child grew up, . . . he became her son. She named him Moses, "because," she said, "I drew him out of the water."

date

Pharaoh's daughter rescued him out of pity. What feelings most often motivate you to help someone in need? What role does your relationship with God play in your actions?

date

date

date

EXODUS 15:19–21

MIRIAM

When the horses of Pharaoh with his chariots and his chariot drivers went into the sea, the LORD brought back the waters of the sea upon them, but the Israelites walked through the sea on dry ground.

Then the prophet Miriam, Aaron's sister, took a tambourine in her hand, and all the women went out after her with tambourines and with dancing. And Miriam sang to them:

"Sing to the LORD, for he has triumphed gloriously;
horse and rider he has thrown into the sea."

date

How do you respond to Miriam's joy at the destruction of the Egyptian army? How does her song fit with God's command to love our neighbors as ourselves?

date

date

date

JOSHUA 2:1, 4

RAHAB

Then Joshua son of Nun sent two men secretly . . . as spies, saying, "Go, view the land, especially Jericho." So they went and entered the house of a prostitute whose name was Rahab and spent the night there. . . . But the woman took the two men and hid them.

date

Why do you think the two spies turned to a prostitute for help? Does their decision impress, amuse, comfort, or dismay you—or provoke some other response? Why?

date

JOSHUA 6:23–25

RAHAB

So the young men who had been spies went in and brought Rahab out, along with . . . all who belonged to her . . . and set them outside the camp of Israel. They [the Israelites] burned down the city and everything in it. . . . But Rahab the prostitute, with her family and all who belonged to her, Joshua spared. . . . For she hid the messengers whom Joshua sent to spy out Jericho.

date

Matthew 1:5 lists Rahab among the ancestors of Jesus. What does God's calling ordinary—or even wicked—people to help carry out God's plans tell you about God?

date

date

date

JUDGES 4:4–5; 5:31

DEBORAH

At that time Deborah, a prophet, . . . was judging Israel. She used to sit under the palm of Deborah . . . , and the Israelites came up to her for judgment. . . . And the land had rest forty years.

date

Deborah was the only female among the twelve judges of Israel. How does your gender affect your relationship with God and the way you carry out your callings?

date

date

date

JUDGES 16:4–6

DELILAH

[Samson] fell in love with a woman . . . whose name was Delilah. The lords of the Philistines came to her and said to her, "Coax him, and find out what makes his strength so great . . . , and we will give you eleven hundred pieces of silver." So Delilah said to Samson, "Please tell me what makes your strength so great and how you could be bound, so that one could subdue you."

date

What does Samson's falling in love with Delilah tell us about him? What does her willingness to betray Samson tell us about her? What is God up to in this story?

date

JUDGES 16:16–17, 19

DELILAH

Finally, after she had nagged him with her words day after day and pestered him, he was tired to death. So he told her his whole secret and said to her, "A razor has never come upon my head. . . . If my head were shaved, then my strength would leave me." . . . She let him fall asleep on her lap, and she called a man and had him shave off the seven locks of his head. He began to weaken, and his strength left him.

date

How does Delilah's successful subterfuge affect your understanding of God? Your relationship with God?

date

date

date

RUTH 1:8–9, 14

NAOMI

But Naomi said to her two daughters-in-law [Orpah and Ruth], "Go back each of you to your mother's house. May the LORD deal kindly with you, as you have dealt with the dead and with me. The LORD grant that you may find security. . . ." Then she kissed them, and they wept aloud. . . . Then . . . Orpah kissed her mother-in-law goodbye, but Ruth clung to her.

date

How do you feel about the blessing Naomi offers her daughters-in-law? What does each woman's choice suggest to you for your own relationships?

date

date

date

RUTH 1:16

RUTH

Ruth said,

"Do not press me to leave you,

to turn back from following you!

Where you go, I will go;

where you lodge, I will lodge;

your people shall be my people

and your God my God."

date

Ruth is included in the gospel of Matthew's genealogy as a forebearer of Jesus. What traits of hers do you see carrying through the family lineage? How do they encourage you in your relationship with God?

date

1 SAMUEL 1:27–28; 1 SAMUEL 2:1

HANNAH

"For this child [Samuel] I prayed, and the LORD has granted me the petition that I made to him. Therefore I have lent him to the LORD; as long as he lives, he is given to the LORD." . . .

Hannah prayed and said,

"My heart exults in the LORD;

my strength is exalted in my God."

date

For what have you prayed—or at least wished—as fervently as Hannah pleaded for a child? What does God's willingness to accept Hannah's loan of her son say to you about God?

date

date

date

2 SAMUEL 11:2, 4

BATHSHEBA

It happened, late one afternoon when David rose from his couch and was walking about on the roof of the king's house, that he saw from the roof a woman [Bathsheba] bathing; the woman was very beautiful. . . . David sent messengers to get her, and she came to him, and he lay with her.

date

Therapists use the term "differential of power" when describing the relationship between people of unequal status. How was that differential a factor in this encounter? Do you think David raped Bathsheba? Why or why not?

date

date

date

2 SAMUEL 11:26–27; 12:15, 24

BATHSHEBA

When [Bathsheba] the wife of Uriah heard that her husband was dead, she made lamentation for him. When the mourning was over, David sent and brought her to his house, and she became his wife and bore him a son. . . . The LORD struck the child whom Uriah's wife bore to David, and it became very ill [and died]. . . . Then David consoled his wife Bathsheba and went to her and lay with her, and she bore a son, and he named him Solomon.

date

What good came out of David's actions? What might Bathsheba have thought and felt about these experiences? Did she see God at work in them? Do you? If so, how?

date

1 KINGS 16:31; 21:25–26

JEZEBEL

He [King Ahab] took as his wife Jezebel. . . . (Indeed, there was no one like Ahab, who sold himself to do what was evil in the sight of the LORD, urged on by his wife Jezebel. He acted most abominably in going after idols.)

date

"Jezebel" has come to refer to any wicked woman. What was at the heart of the evil that both Jezebel and Ahab committed? How might such evil be manifest today?

date

date

date

2 KINGS 9:34–35

JEZEBEL

Then he [King Jehu] went in and ate and drank; he said, "See to that cursed woman and bury her, for she is a king's daughter." But when they went out to bury her, they found no more than her skull and the feet and the palms of her hands.

date

Jezebel's death is one of the most gruesome narrated in the Bible. Why did the storyteller include these details? How do they affect the way you think and feel about Jezebel? About God?

date

date

date

ESTHER 1:10–12, 21–22

VASHTI

He [King Ahasuerus] commanded . . . the seven eunuchs who attended him to bring Queen Vashti before the king wearing the royal crown, in order to show the peoples and the officials her beauty. . . . But Queen Vashti refused to come. . . . At this the king was enraged. . . . And the king . . . sent letters to all the royal provinces, declaring that every man should be master in his own house.

date

Why might Queen Vashti have refused her husband's command? Do you find yourself cheering her on for her determination or shaking your head at her stubbornness? How does the king's declaration strike you?

date

ESTHER 2:2–4

ESTHER

Then the king's servants who attended him said, ". . . Let the king appoint commissioners in all the provinces of his kingdom to gather all the beautiful young virgins. . . . And let the young woman who pleases the king be queen instead of Vashti."

date

"God" is never mentioned in the book of Esther. In what ways do you nonetheless see God at work in this story? What do you learn about God from these actions?

date

date

date

ESTHER 2:8–10

ESTHER

When the king's order and his edict were proclaimed and when many young women were gathered . . . , Esther was taken into the king's palace. . . . The young woman pleased him and won his favor. . . . Esther did not reveal her [Jewish] people or kindred, for [her uncle] Mordecai had charged her not to tell.

date

Imagine yourself in Esther's position. How might she have felt about keeping a secret from the king? From him as her husband? Have secrets affected any of your important relationships? If so, how?

date

date

date

ESTHER 3:13; 4:4

ESTHER

Letters were sent by couriers to all the king's provinces, giving orders to destroy, to kill, and to annihilate all Jews, young and old, children and women, in one day . . . and to plunder their goods. . . . When Esther's maids and her eunuchs came and told her, the queen was deeply distressed.

date

Although God is not mentioned in the book of Esther, how might the Jews' status as God's chosen have led them to see God's hand in this story? Where do you see God at work in your own life?

date

ESTHER 4:13–14

ESTHER

Mordecai told them [the king's eunuchs] to reply to Esther, . . . "For if you keep silent at this time, relief and deliverance will rise for the Jews from another place, but you and your father's family will perish. Who knows? Perhaps you have come to royal dignity for just such a time as this."

date

What "royal dignity" has been given to you? How does thinking of yourself as chosen by God affect the way you carry out your callings?

date

date

date

ESTHER 9:20, 22, 32

ESTHER

Mordecai recorded these things and sent letters to all the Jews who were in all the provinces of King Ahasuerus, . . . that they should make them days of feasting and gladness, days for sending gifts of food to one another and presents to the poor. . . . The command of Esther fixed these practices of Purim, and it was recorded in writing.

date

What was the source of Esther's power? How could you use your power to help others?

date

date

date